JUMPING THE

THE

Q

A Total Quality Perspective

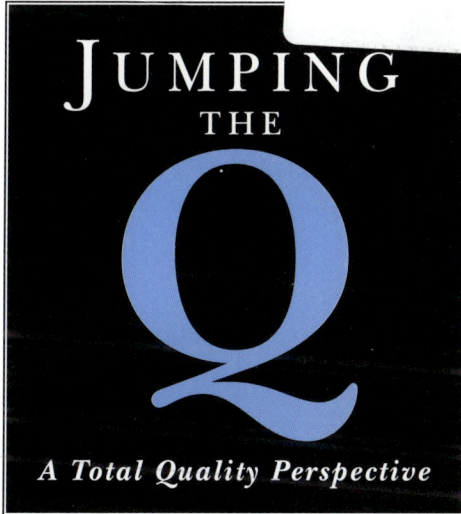

Headway · Hodder & Stoughton

British Library Cataloguing in Publication Data
A catalogue for this book is held with the British Library

ISBN 0 340 60754 8

First published 1994
Impression number 10 9 8 7 6 5 4 3 2 1
Year 1998 1997 1996 1995 1994

Acknowledgements

Thanks are due to many people. In particular, to James Bentley and Paul Mills of KPMG's Centre for Manufacturing and Logistics Consultancy for having the faith to sponsor the writing of this book; to my colleague Graham Oddey for his creativity and innate understanding of the subject; to Barbara Zanditon for having the vision and tenacity necessary to find the right publisher; and to Tim Gregson-Williams of Hodder Headline for his support and wise counsel. And finally, to Alan Paterson of Butcher Patterson for the enormous contribution he made to the preparation of the text. Alan is that true rarity, a man who really knows how to exploit successfully what he is genuinely good at. Find people you can trust. Trust them.

OWEN BULL
August 1993, Birmingham

Q

"Something much more than mere means of transport...

is necessary if an army is to be impelled into rapid forward motion. The army needs a vision, a dream, a nightmare, or some mixture of the three if it is to be electrified into a headlong advance."

JOHN KEEGAN, *The Face of Battle: Study of Agincourt, Waterloo and the Somme* (1976) Hutchinson.

Q

Why?

Jumping the Q

Q

- Why Total Quality?

- Why do you want to know?

- On the face of it, asking 'why' may appear facetious.

- It's obvious. Our costs are too high, our output is too low, our products and services aren't selling. Our very survival is at stake.

- So what do you expect from Total Quality?

- A sudden injection of adrenaline that'll catapult your organisation into the ranks of the 'globally competitive' (whatever that means)?

- Why do you think that?

- Why are you interested in TQ?

- Why are you reading this book?

Q

Why?

Desparately seeking reason

Q   *Why?*
Because you want to serve your customers better?

Q   *Why?*
Because you want to reduce your costs?

Q   *Why?*
Because you want to achieve real, sustainable competitive advantage?

Q   *Why?*
Because you want to improve employee relations?

Q   *Why?*

Is this labouring the point? Perhaps. But we think not. TQ has been around for a decade or more, and is credited with a number of successes: Toyota, Motorola, ICL, Land Rover. The names are familiar, but thin on the ground, because for every 'Quality Company' glowing with the pride that accompanies success, there are a dozen would-be TQers smouldering with the resentment of shattered hopes. Total Quality, it is increasingly suggested, is a bust. It all *sounds* great. Problem is, it just doesn't seem to work.

Perhaps, just perhaps, one key difference between the successful and unsuccessful 'wannabes', is that the unsuccessful ones tried erecting the superstructure without first ensuring that the foundations were solid.

Total Quality means bringing about a fundamental culture change within an organisation. The foundation of the new culture has to be the faith that there is a better way of doing things, and that we are really fully committed to it. And ultimately, if the people of the organisation are to buy into this new faith, the people selling it to them have to believe themselves. *Really* believe. They have to be absolutely sure in their own minds that they *know* the answer to the most fundamental question of all:

why?

Q

why?

Got an answer?

So far so good.

But there's a long way to go. An answer, after all, ends with a full stop.

Finish.

The end.

We're barely past the beginning.

So here are some questions, to go with your answer.

Q Would your answer be applauded by your customers?

Q Would it be applauded by your shareholders?

Q Would it be applauded by your workforce, your bankers, and your suppliers?

Q Would it, in short, be applauded by *all* those who are, in one way or another, stakeholders in your business?

Be honest.

Here's why:

Unless your answer to the question 'why' would be endorsed, with unqualified enthusiasm, by all your stakeholders, it is not the answer you need.

Could you come up with a single speech, explaining your reasons, which would attract the applause of a hall full of customers, or a hall full of employees, or a hall full of shareholders? Trickier still, with a hall filled with a random selection of stakeholders from all key categories? If not, think again.

It's infernally difficult, and it demands a complex balancing act far more subtle than the 'buy cheap, sell dear' philosophy which underpinned yesterday's commercial organisation. But if you cannot achieve it, you're in trouble.

You *have* to ask yourself:

why?

Q

"May I tell him who's furious?"

Jumping the Q

Q

What?

Q

Q

"What the hell is Quality? What is it?

"And what is good, Phaedrus,

and what is not good –

need we ask anyone to tell us these things?"

ROBERT PIRSIG, *Zen and the Art of Motorcycle Maintenance* (1991)
Bodley Head

Q

What is total quality?

—

- **TQ is not a science.**

- **TQ is not a prescribed, precise, definitive system.**

- **TQ is a collection of half-baked ideas.**

- **You have a problem with that?**

- **Don't you have an oven?**

'Half-baked' is generally used as a term of abuse. In this case, however, it's used to drive home the essential fact that Total Quality is derived from many sources and includes many ideas which may be more or less applicable to the particular situation your company finds itself in. Crudely, what worked for Toyota in the mid-70s may or may not be right for your organisation as we approach the twenty-first century.

If you expect an off-the-shelf guarantee of enhanced performance, you're heading for a disappointment. The half-baked ideas that constitute Total Quality first need combining in a recipe that's right for your company and then finishing off in your oven – preferably a microwave oven – to ensure even cooking, right the way through.

Total Quality is a more-or-less agreed set of ingredients. The precise recipe you use, the particular dish you prepare, depends on you, your company, and your oven.

Got your oven ready? Here are a few ingredients...

Q

Still searching for excellence

—

"... to our initial surprise, the content of the culture was invariably limited to just a handful of themes. Whether bending tin, frying hamburgers, or providing rooms for rent, virtually all of the excellent companies had, it seemed, defined themselves as de facto service businesses. Customers reign supreme. They are not treated to untested technology or unnecessary goldplating. They are the recipients of products that last, service delivered promptly."

Excerpt taken from *In Search of Excellence* by THOMAS J. PETERS and ROBERT H. WATERMAN JNR. Copyright © 1982 Thomas J. Peters and Robert H. Waterman Jnr. Reprinted by permission of HarperCollins Publishers Inc.

After *In Search of Excellence,* management theory was never the same again. At a stroke, the MBAs and statisticians and spreadsheet analysts were shunted off into the wings, and 'The Customer' moved centre stage.

If the customer was the star of the new production, the employee was the co-star. Business, it was declared, was no longer about numbers, or computers, or long-term strategy – it was about people serving people.

Nothing has really changed since: businesses are still seeking strategies for survival, and customers are still seeking products that last and service that's delivered promptly.

Ideas don't have to be new to be good. They just have to be good.

...After **In Search of Excellence,** *management theory was never the same again...*

Q

The Customer: not a king; not a god

If you really wanted to describe Total Quality in a single catch-all phrase, it would have to be that adopting Total Quality means adopting a customer-oriented business strategy. It doesn't negate the need for an IT strategy, or a human resources strategy, or a marketing strategy, or any number of other strategies – but it puts them in their place. *All* business strategies are to be subordinated to *one* overriding criterion: customer-orientation. However, some bizarre ideas have been derived from this basic, and valid, proposition.

'The Customer is King', for example: surely one of the most asinine slogans to have come out of recent management theory. The customer is *not* a king. If he was, he would have flunkies to do his shopping.

The deification of the customer has us all mesmerised. We are all customers, and we know full well that there are times when we are not right. Whoever said 'the customer is always right' never served behind a shop counter. Sometimes the customer is a right royal pain in the backside.

Demanding of your people that they take an abject stance when confronted by a customer is no way to achieve good customer service. Your people have their integrity; they are as deserving of respect as your customers. The basic rule should be 'civility, but not servility'. A meeting of employee and customer should be a meeting of equals: two human beings, equally deserving of respect.

You shouldn't ask your staff to prostrate themselves before the great god customer; 'do as you would be done by' is quite adequate. It's also more realistic.

Many businesses operate – or try to operate – on the assumption that all their employees are imperfect and all their customers are perfect. This is, of course, palpable nonsense. Most employees and most customers are ordinary, decent people: they don't ask to be treated like kings, nor like crooks, just as human beings, deserving of the respect that's accorded to human beings simply by virtue of their humanity.

Q

Total Competence

—

"Do the common thing uncommonly well"

PAUL OREFFICE, Chairman, Dow Chemical

Indeed. The customer neither is nor claims to be a king. Nor does the customer ask or expect to be treated regally. In many market sectors, customers aren't concerned about 'excellence'; they're still waiting for competence.

Competence means things like doing what you say you will do. People judge your organisation by criteria such as: if they say they will ring me back, do they? If they say they will confirm it in writing, does a letter appear? Are their bills itemised, so that I know exactly what I'm paying for?

Most of the things people actually want are pretty basic.

Many large financial organisations spent the 80s in a haze of global megalomania, overlooking the potential closer to home. Right on their own doorstep, their customers – and their competitors' customers – were still waiting to be offered basic services with a basic level of competence. Even now, as financial institutions turn to large-scale advertising to try to improve their image and reputation, the pubs and dinner tables of Britain still resound with, 'well that's nothing compared to what my bank did to *me*' stories. Imagine if people started telling 'what my bank did *for* me' stories...

I am the customer. I don't want people parroting 'have a nice day' at me – it embarrasses me. What I want in the first instance is an acceptable product or service at a fair price; nothing more fancy than that.

I like courtesy. Not humility, just ordinary common or garden politeness.

I like it when people make the effort to remember my name, and to use it when they deal with me.

I like it when I have a problem, and ring up to arrange for it to be dealt with, and find myself talking to someone who gives the impression that they care, and that they will do what's necessary to deal with it.

One large utility company initiated a quality drive by asking each employee to list 'three things that drive our customers crazy'. Simple, basic, effective.

Q

"Which do you recommend – the one with the high running costs, the brand that is electrically unsafe and difficult to service, or the one with the poor finish and unreliable thermostat?"

One step beyond...

Competence gets you to the starting line. Being the first across the winning line, though – particularly in a global market – demands something more. If satisfying the customer is the new global benchmark to survive, *delighting* the customer is what allows you to thrive. Sounds weird? What about when *you* are a customer: can you remember ever being delighted, and how delighted you were about it?

Crudely expressed, the traditional company tends to be 'us-driven' rather than customer-led. The organisation develops its products and services and then goes about trying to identify the customer needs they might be used to meet.

The Total Quality company, by contrast, turns that basic development process on its head: it starts out by clearly identifying its customers' actual needs and then develops appropriate solutions to meet them.

So far so good. But the real Quality companies, it appears, take that basic approach one stage further: they aim not only to meet customers' needs, but to *anticipate,* even *create* needs, giving their customers not only what they want, but what they *didn't even know they wanted*.

The Range Rover spawned a whole new market for luxurious off-road vehicles. It was, and remains, 'the car nobody thought of but everyone wanted.' The new need – the new niche – was created by the company.

Leading supermarkets now sell packets of ready-grated carrots, at well over £1 a pound, while yards away fresh carrots are on sale for 20p a pound. In other words, the chains have found a way to take raw materials and 'add value' to such an extent that products incorporating mark-ups of several hundred per cent are not only acceptable to the customer, but positively welcomed.

What's more, anticipating new needs is increasingly an essential element in any successful company's strategy, simply because the survival benchmarks are constantly shifting. Think of the reliability of a modern £10 000 car: far better than that of the £20 000 car of a couple of decades ago.

Even for the companies which successfully anticipate or create new customer demands, satisfying existing ones is still the bedrock on which their success is founded. Nevertheless, thinking one step ahead, going one step beyond, is essential for any organisation wishing to 'jump the queue', to become the best.

Fundamental: going a step beyond means thinking a step ahead. And what's the source of thinking, of inspiration, of innovation? People.

Q

Still searching for excellence

—

"Wittgenstein always had a keen appreciation of sound work-manship and a genuinely moral disapproval of the flimsy or slip-shod. He liked to think that there might be craftsmen who would insist on doing their jobs to perfection and for no reason other than that was the way it ought to be."

NORMAN MALCOLM, *Ludwig Wittgenstein – A Memoir* (1958) by permission of
Oxford University Press.

It has been held as a fundamental of Total Quality theory that quality is in the eye of the beholder, that it is the verdict of the buyer that lays down the criteria for product or service performance. It's a strong and valid principle, which certainly rules out many absurdities from business, a classical example of which is investing vast sums perfecting a product that turns out to be something no one wants to buy.

Yet, as so often, many of the most successful companies seem to have, as it were, gone beyond this conventional wisdom. Many seem to have created a climate in which something akin to 'art for art's sake' is fostered and encouraged. Ray Kroc, of McDonald's, for example, spent a fortune on Research and Development not to create a hamburger that the American public would find acceptable, but to create the finest hamburger it was possible for human beings to create.

But in many ways, this kind of passion, this attention to detail, is in fact more in tune with the basic philosophy of Total Quality than the apparently more pragmatic injunction to produce 'the quality the market actually demands'. It's hard to imagine people getting fired up over a mission to produce a hamburger that consistently meets customer requirements, but ask them to help create 'the best damn hamburger in the world', and they've really got something to get their teeth into.

> *"The Japanese take perfection, or at least the pursuit of it, as a matter of fact. Toyota has a test track on the north island of Hokkaido. One of the facilities there is a stretch of road four kilometres long which is perfectly flat. This is used to test certain dynamic characteristics of vehicles. The only variation on the notion of perfect flatness is that the road's surface dips by 18 mm in the centre, to compensate for the curvature of the earth."*
>
> STEPHEN BAYLEY. *'Expression' Magazine* (American Express)

The heroes of Total Quality businesses tend to be *perfectionists*. They can't help it; it's just the way they're built.

Q

Giant leap versus continuous improvement

—

Traditional theory has it that while we in the West concentrate on looking for 'The Big Idea' that will suddenly leap-frog the competition and put us ahead of the game, the more diligent, disciplined and level-headed citizens of the Pacific Rim concentrate instead on so-called Kaizen, which translates roughly as 'continuous improvement'.

Kaizen basically says that looking for the giant leap is all well and good; but the essential key to achieving and maintaining competitive advantage is to have every single person in the organisation trying to do whatever they do a little bit better every day. The cumulative effect of an infinite number of tiny incremental improvements originated by everyone, will exceed the effect of any individual idea or initiative, no matter how grand or impressive.

But where does that leave us in the West?

Japan was able to overtake the West through following the principles of Kaizen, because incremental improvement confronted virtual stagnation. Little by little, the tortoise caught up not with the hare, but with a slug. Now the tortoise is steadily picking up speed.

Does it actually make sense for us – faced with this ever-receding winning line – to try to employ the practices which worked in the past for another nation facing a fundamentally different competitive situation? How, to put it bluntly, will incremental improvement enable us to catch up with competitors who are *themselves* incrementally improving? Can we not just do it, but do it faster?

The answer, perhaps, is two-fold: first, in many business sectors we are not confronting competition from the Pacific Basin, and in such areas, the first to adopt Kaizen successfully will effectively overtake competitors who don't; second, global standards are *already* being set by some Western companies. Some European car manufacturers, for example, such as Rover and Ford, rather than simply adopting Japanese systems off the shelf, have *adapted* those systems to create a unique Euro-system which suits their existing culture and capabilities, and are in the process of becoming the pace-setters.

Adopt Kaizen from the East, combine it with traditional Western capacity for 'The Big Idea', and you get a new synthesis representing the best of both worlds.

Q

Total win/win

"Good business should contain something for both parties."

JOHN HARVEY-JONES, *Making It Happen* (1988) Fontana, an imprint of
HarperCollins Publishers Ltd.

Good business, in fact, should contain something for *all* parties.

A number of interest groups combine in a company: investors, employees, financiers, suppliers, customers... Traditionally, companies have aimed to profit-maximise, and they do this at the expense of other stakeholders. Is this what it's all about?

The question is worth a good hard think, because the Quality companies seem to have thrived by flying in the face of this conventional wisdom: somehow, they seem to have squared the circle. Such companies differ in an infinite variety of ways, but they have one thing in common: a belief that in the long run, success seems to come when you manage to run things in a way that benefits not one party, but *all* parties. This approach lies at the heart of what TQ is all about.

They've discovered that while you might be able to make a quick buck by fleecing your customers or exploiting your workforce, sustainable success, growth, and long-term profitability come when you give customers a good deal at a fair price, and pay people a fair day's pay for a fair day's work. It's not a question of altruism or niceness, it's a question of hard-headed, commercial, pragmatic self-interest that can see beyond the end of its nose.

In the Total Quality company, everyone's a winner. It's the profit-maximising competition that loses; squabbling over today's spoils, it fundamentally undermines the foundations for tomorrow's.

'Fair play' isn't just fair, it seems, but the one sure route to sustainable success.

Q

The best leaders do little but lead

—

Ray Kroc was, without doubt, one of the true visionaries of the twentieth century. And it is, perhaps, the ultimate testament to his greatness that when he left the scene, McDonald's didn't miss a beat.

Mediocre managers are invariably indispensable. They arrive at the office early and leave late. They take work home with them. They come in over the weekend. They refuse to take their holiday entitlement. They refuse to take time off when they're ill, because they're *so* important. They would blanche at any suggestion that work should be enjoyable, or fun. Call it masochism management; call it macho management: by any name, it's bad management.

Even a patrol leader in the scouts knows that the first skill of management is the ability to delegate. He may be the best in his patrol at tying knots, building rafts and putting up tents, but even if he is, he can't tie every knot, or make rafts and erect tents on his own. There's just too much to do, and if he tries to do it all himself, he's going to end up as a basket case while his charges stand around bored witless or court approaches from the devil who, as ever, is fully capable of supplying work for idle hands to do...

One test of leadership is the ability of the led unit to function effectively in the absence of its leader. The good commanding officer in wartime is not the one who is essential to the functioning of his troops, but the one whose troops will continue to press home the attack effectively even if he falls.

In his book, *Moments of Truth* (1989), Jan Carlzon, CEO of Scandinavian Airlines, sums up the paradox at the heart of the notion of leadership. He tells of his first attempt to take a holiday, frustrated by a constantly ringing telephone. Before he next takes a holiday, he gives an interview to a newspaper in which he expresses his conviction that he has appointed managers to manage – not to defer to him over every decision that needs taking. The message gets through:

> *"A few days later I left for vacation. And for four weeks the telephone remained wonderfully silent."*

This, perhaps, is the ultimate test of leadership. Not the ability to make the right decisions, but the ability to supply a vision powerful enough to guide, sustain and coordinate the efforts of all a company's people. Think of the leader of a struggling company as a corporate psychiatrist: the mark of ultimate success is when the doctor can turn to the patient and say, 'you don't need me any more'.

"He likes to make business fun."

Q

How?

Q

"The journey of a thousand miles begins with a single step"

LAO TZU quoted by JOHN HEIDER. *The Tao of Leadership*
(1993) Gower Publishing Group

"If you cry 'forward!' you must without fail make plain in which direction to go. Don't you see that if, without doing so, you call out the word to both a monk and revolutionary, they will go in directions precisely opposite?"

ANTON CHEKOV

How do you do TQ?

- You start out.

- You keep going.

- And going, and going, and going.

- And you never, ever, stop.

Q

"Where there is no vision..."

—

"Where there is no vision, the people perish."

The Book of Revelations

Strategy or tactics?

The debate rolls on from year to year. The strategists accuse the tacticians of lack of vision; the tacticians retort that the strategists are busy building castles in the sky. Any halfway sane observer can only conclude that the divide is a false one – that strategy and tactics are inextricably intertwined, that the 'what' can only work through the medium of the 'how'. And underpinning both, ultimately, is the 'why'.

The 'why' dictates the 'what'.

The 'what' dictates the 'how'.

Every business needs a reason, a mission, a vision. Without it, strategy and tactics are impotent. You need many things for a successful journey – transport, supplies, a route, travelling companions, but all of these are redundant if you lack the one thing no journey can be without: a destination.

There's an anecdote which, through overuse in management theories, is beginning to get a bit dog-eared, but it bears repetition. Most clichés become clichés because they express some simple, universal truth... so here goes.

Two men are hacking away at the rock face in a quarry. A stranger comes by, and asks them what they're up to. The first looks bored and tired, and says, 'I'm cutting this rock into regular slabs'; the second, cheerful and enthusiastic, says, 'I'm part of a team that's building a cathedral'.

> *"I think most of us are looking for a calling, not a job. Most of us, like the assembly-line worker, have jobs that are too small for our spirit. Jobs are not big enough for people."*

Worker quoted in STUDS TERKEL's *Working* Copyright © 1972, 1974 Studs Terkel. Reprinted with permission from Pantheon Books.

It's not what people *do*, necessarily, that makes the difference between 'a calling' and mindless drudgery: it's how they *see* what they do. It's a question of vision.

Q

Find people you can trust: trust them

"Ultimately, whatever the form of economic activity, it is people that count most."

LORD SIEFF, *On Management: Marks & Spencer Way* (1990)
by permission of Weidenfeld and Nicolson

Marks & Spencer is renowned for the way it treats its people. And itdoesn't do this purely to satisfy altruistic ideals. Long ago it recognised that there are hard business benefits to be gained from such an approach. Put simply, treat your people well and they respond with improved efficiency, which means better products and services. And better products and services lead to increased sales and profits.

So how do you do it?

The key, it seems, is to make clear to your people what you want from them, then give them the power and the tools to do the job, and let them get on with it. Trust them. Get the best out of them, but not in an uncaring, exploitative way, which makes them fearful and resentful, and will eventually drive them out of the company. Rather, as Anita Roddick of The Body Shop has found, do it in a way which inspires them:

"What I have learned is that people become motivated when you guide them to the source of their own power and when you make heroes out of employees who personify what you want to see in the organisation."

ANITA RODDICK, *Body and Soul: How to succeed in Business and Change the World* (1992)
Vermillion, an imprint of the Random House (UK) Group

Does it work?

Emphatically yes. Look at Virgin. Richard Branson delegates tasks and responsibilities to people who often do not seem to have the appropriate experience. In his book *Richard Branson – The Inside Story* (1989), Mick Brown cites the example of how, in the early days Branson would turn record-packers into talent scouts and magazine salesmen into managers. Not only did this work well, it also resulted in his trust being repaid with tremendous loyalty and dedication.

Find people you can trust. Trust them. After all, if you don't, why should they trust you?

Q

*"Keep up the good work, whatever it is,
whoever you are."*

Q

What do your people need?

—

"My own experience of trying to teach and train managers is that it is extremely difficult to teach grown-up people anything. It is, however, relatively easy to create conditions under which people will train themselves."

JOHN HARVEY-JONES, *Making it happen* (1988) Fontana, an imprint of Harper Collins Publishers Ltd.

Traditional TQ theory lays great store by training. Don't invest in technology; invest in people. After all, the first rule of technology is 'garbage in; garbage out', and input is 100 per cent human. Plus, what makes for commercial success and adaptability in a fast-changing commercial climate is your company's capacity to generate ideas. And only people have ideas.

Tom Peters likes to quote the example of the sausage factory in the mid-west of America, whose policy on training is simple: any worker can take any training on any subject – job-related or not – and the company foots the bill. How can a company in a definitive low-margin industry afford it? Altruism? No. The theory is simple: if you're learning, you're an engaged and alive human being; and engaged and alive human beings make better sausages.

It's all hard to dispute. But rushing into mass off-the-shelf training programmes can be a classic way of putting the cart before the horse. All too often, the employee's response is, 'damn it, I don't have time to go back to school to learn about this "flavour of the month" called Total Quality – I've got a job to do.'

Better, by far, to grab the guys from the paintshop and get *them* to address the evidence of 'global best practice' – so that they can really *see* what the best looks like. Then the guys at the paintshop are going to take it personally. They're going to think, 'hey, our cars are really bad', and they're going to start asking 'why can't *we* get a finish like that?' And once they take ownership of the real issue at stake – improving the finish on the cars, rather than, say, learning about Statistical Process Control – they'll be ready to listen to someone who explains that the way your competitor gets a finish like that is because all *their* paintshop guys know what an Ishikawa diagram is. They're going to say, 'well how can *we* learn what an Ishikawa diagram is?' Where there's a will there's a way. But the will must come first.

In any case, for the most part your people already know what they need to give the customer a better deal. What they need most of all is a boss who's willing to listen, and come through with *whatever* it takes, whether training, technology, flexitime or a creche.

Total respect

—

"The [prestige car] showroom was divided into two sections, with separate unmarked doors. I entered the first, and asked the receptionist whether this was the new or used sales department. 'What are the registration letters on the cars?' was her curt reply, setting the tone for the visit."

Performance Car magazine, August 1992

How do you get your people to work together well to treat your customers well? Easy. Treat *them* well. Try being *kind* to your people. 'Kind? What's kindness got to do with business?' The word 'kind' is closely linked to the words 'kin' and 'kindred'. In successful companies, people feel kinship with their colleagues. If the prevailing atmosphere isn't one of kindred spirits working together, you'd better watch out – because in the successful companies, it is.

Customers like dealing with people who are alive and interested, positive and cheerful. But how many people feel like that, if they're being treated as dispensable wage-slaves? How can you expect one group of people to treat another group of people with respect if they

themselves are being treated with disrespect? The first and fundamental rule of customer service is this:

As you treat your people, so your people will treat your customers.

After all, if you really *do* believe in giving good customer service, surely you believe equally in giving good employee service? Strange con-
cept? You don't exist to serve your employees? You think your
employees are there to serve you? Surely they are there to serve your
customers...

> *"Rude and ignorant shop assistants are the worst feature of
> shopping, according to a survey commissioned by the National
> Consumer Council. In a survey by MORI of nearly 2 000 peo-
> ple, 43 per cent expressed some dissatisfaction. Staff were most
> often described as unhelpful, uninterested, rude and ignorant."*

The Guardian, 30 July 1992

Do you suppose those staff are unhelpful, uninterested, rude and
ignorant at home? If not, what goes wrong when they come to work?
And isn't really thinking about that question likely to prove a more
fruitful way to improve customer service than sticking up supposedly
motivational posters on the walls?

Q

Personal initiative versus corporate discipline

—

"The fundamental secret to McDonald's success is the way it achieves uniformity and allegiance to an operating regimen without sacrificing the strength of American individuality and creativity."

JOHN F. LOVE, *McDonald's Behind the Arches*, copyright © 1986 John F. Love. Used by permission of Bantam Books, a division of Bantam Doubleday Dell Publishing Group Inc.

Traditional TQ theory sets great store by 'empowering your people'. Theorists quote with approval initiatives such as Nordstrom's employee rulebook which contains just one rule: 'Use your own best judgement in all situations.'

Then you come across McDonald's – surely a quality company par excellence – which as a 600-page policy document, weighing four pounds, which lays out *exactly* what the employee has to do in every conceivable situation, from where to put patties on the grill to the frequency of window washing.

So what's the story? Do you tell people what to do, or leave it to their best judgement? It depends.

In McDonald's, and many similar organisations, it's neither rigid conformity nor everyone doing their own thing. Rather, it's about devising a system or amending the process continuously in a way which eradicates failure and wastage, and thus focuses all resources on meeting customer needs.

There are two vital corollaries to this, i.e. that everyone *follows the system*, as prescribed, but also, importantly, that everyone *contributes to improving the system*: successful innovations are incorporated on an ongoing basis, to form the new, better system, which is then followed in a disciplined way by everyone.

In the Nordstroms of this world, there is no 'system', as such.

It depends, ultimately, on *what matters to the customer*. Nordstrom customers want personal, attentive, knowledgable assistance; McDonald's customers want a hot, tasty burger, quickly, and at a reasonable price. For the first, you need empowered employees, for the second, you need rigid adherence to a strict operating regimen which rules out the potential for human error, and thus delivers a product which meets specifications with absolute consistency.

"So I gave it to him straight, I did – In a time of recession, go for expansion, borrow, re-equip and fight back, I said..."

Reproduced by permission of Punch.

Q

Centralisation is not a dirty word

—

Having established that there's no single, definitive, universally applicable answer to the questions, 'how far do we go in empowering our people, and to what extent do we impose uniformity?', we have to address an analogous structural issue.

Over recent years, management gurus have declared open war on centralisation in organisations. 'Devolve, devolve!' goes up the cry.

Take out the head office bureaucrats and give your people the autonomy they need to serve the customers they deal with.

Sounds fine and dandy. But is it really that simple? Centralisation bad; devolution good?

In fact, while the underlying drivers of such general principles may be appealing, things are a bit more complicated than that. *All* businesses need a degree of centralisation, and a degree of local autonomy. How to find the balance? As with people, so with corporate functions: you have to ask yourself what actually determines the experience your customers enjoy – or don't – when they deal with your company. Which involves not simply the individual, one-on-one buying experience, but the entire package which constitutes that buying experience. Which, in turn, includes matters like price, and predictability, as well as personalisation.

Put simply, local autonomy is the key to personalised service: treating each customer as an individual, unique human being. Yet it can also be the enemy of efficiency and consistency which, in some cases, are valued more highly by the customer than personalised service. Take McDonald's, again, to make the point:

> *"The Chicago franchiser insisted on nearly complete control over certain tasks – enforcing operating rules, training, designing equipment and financing – which benefit most from centralisation and standardisation. Yet it was giving its franchisees enormous freedom to work on those tasks – advertising, promotion, and new product development – where the operator's proximity to the consumer was a definite advantage."*

To hear some theorists, you'd think Total Quality was all about 'setting your people *free*!' It would be nice if life were so simple; but it isn't. Centralise what should be centralised; devolve where appropriate, and to the appropriate level. Once again, there's no single, simple answer: you have to use your brain.

Total efficiency

"If pure water flows from the upper stream, there is no need to purify it further downstream."

HIROTO KAGAMI, © International Management, (1993) Reed Business Publishing

One of the outstanding success stories of recent years has been The Body Shop, set up by Anita and Gordon Roddick. And when you look at how their success has come about, you find that much of it is attributable to rigorous adherence to some simple, basic, common sense principles. For example:

"Gordon and I have never lost the sense of outrage we felt at the beginning when we thought we were being misused, or our time and money were being wasted... Cutting down waste is no more than good housekeeping."

Anita Roddick, *Body and Soul*, Vermillion

Waste. Eliminating it is a large part of Total Quality. People like Anita Roddick are obsessive in their desire to cut out waste. But lest you think such people are a phenomenon of our times, consider the case of Henry Ford.

Henry Ford has become something of a bogey man in modern management theory. He dehumanised his factories; he wouldn't make colourful cars. He laid, it is said, the seeds of the decline of Western industry. But there's a real danger of throwing out the baby with the bathwater. Because much of what Ford preached and practised is as valid today as it ever was. He loathed waste.

To eliminate waste you have to find out what causes it. To find out what causes it you have to understand the process which produces it.

Seventy years ago, Henry Ford wrote:

> *"Where most manufacturers find themselves quicker to make a change in the product than in the method of manufacturing – we follow exactly the opposite course... Our big changes have been in methods of manufacturing. They never stand still. I believe that there is hardly a single operation in the making of our car that is the same as when we made our first car of the present model. That is why we make them so cheaply."*
>
> Henry Ford, *My Life and Work*, Doubleday

Very often, the changes introduced were so marginal as to appear insignificant: line heights were adjusted to the quarter-inch; their speed to the second; their position to use every last scrap of space. Bit by bit, minute by minute, cent by cent and inch by inch, wasted motion and misspent energy were squeezed out of the production process.

No one did more to advance the use of technology, or to eradicate waste. Nevertheless, as Henry discovered to his cost, eradicating waste is necessary, but not sufficient. When you buy productivity at the expense of people, you're heading for trouble...

Q

Total integration

—

> *"What I found at Chrysler were thirty-five vice presidents, each with his own turf. There was no real committee setup, no cement in the organisational chart, no system of meetings to get people talking to each other. I couldn't believe, for example, that the guy running the engineering department wasn't in constant touch with his counterpart in manufacturing. But that's how it was. Everybody worked independently. I took one look at the system and I almost threw up. That's when I knew I was in really deep trouble."*
>
> LEE IACOCCA, *Iacocca – An Autobiography*, Sedgewick and Jackson

What Iacocca found at Chrysler is nothing unusual. All too often we see sales departments not talking to manufacturing. People in manufacturing seeing their job as making products. People in sales seeing their job as selling products. And never the twain shall meet.

And in the yards and the warehouses from Detroit to Dagenham, the results are all too visible: acre upon acre of unsold output. Inventory. Non-working capital. Non-working capital rusting bit by bit by bit.

Often this lack of communication between departments doesn't have visible results. Most of the time, you simply find a situation where people defend their turf against allcomers, considering any suggestions from 'Them' – i.e. anyone from another department – as impertinence. Things go missing, ideas get lost, frustrations build, people find themselves unable to do their jobs properly, animosities grow, and feed on themselves; in a thousand tiny, often almost invisible ways, the energy, drive and enthusiasm of the people in the company is leeched away into sheer frustration, while the company goes gently down the pan.

People are by their nature social beings. They will naturally form themselves into some kind of 'Us', to which they will become intensely loyal. If you leave the question of what constitutes 'Us' to entirely random processes, you will find the front-line despising the backroom pen-pushers, the design department hating the engineers, and everyone loathing senior management.

'Us', within a company, has to mean 'Us – the company'. Any more localised loyalties than that, and you can forget any hope of having the company working together to satisfy customers.

Q

*"No doubt some of you have never participated
in a shoot-out before."*

Q

Total teamwork

When people see the word 'team' their spirits sink. Please God we're not going to have Quality Circles, or start each day with calisthenics and a rousing rendition of the company song. Please God.

There's an underlying gut fear at work: the fear that we're about to be subjected to some kind of weird oriental 'clonery' – that our individuality is about to be suppressed 'for the greater good'. But in fact there's nothing bizarre or inherently 'foreign' about teamwork. Especially not in a country which gave the world soccer, rugby, cricket, and pretty much every other game the world plays. Teamwork is no more and no less than working together with one or more other people to try to achieve something. Nothing so weird about that.

As with many other aspects of Total Quality, the key to successful teamwork is Tom Peters' fundamental dynamic duo: system and passion. Team members have to know *how* to go about working together effectively toward achieving their prescribed objectives; and they must also have the verve, the zest and the enthusiasm – as a group – to motivate them to put those capabilities to work.

Harvey Mackay, writing in *Beware The Naked Man Who Offers You His Shirt*, quotes football coach Lou Holtz who, arriving at a new club, distributed T-shirts with the word TEAM in large brash capitals, and the word 'me' in much smaller type underneath. Yet teams succeed not when their members suppress their individuality, but when they assert it fully, while encouraging and helping their fellow team members to do likewise, under an overriding conviction that all are involved in, to quote the great B-movie line, 'something that's bigger than both of us'. Or, more often 'all of us'.

But what's the key to achieving such group motivation? Iacocca again, quoting another football coach Vince Lombardi...

> *"...if you're going to play together as a team, you've got to care for one another. You've got to love each other... The difference between mediocrity and greatness... is the feeling these guys have for each other. Most people call it team spirit. When the players are imbued with that special feeling, you know you've got yourself a winning team."*
>
> LEE IACOCCA, *Iacocca – An Autobiography*, Sedgewick and Jackson

The ability, the drive, plus the magic ingredient called 'team spirit', which Vince Lombardi – no new-age radical, but one of the hardest men ever to prowl a touchline – accounts for using words like 'care', 'feeling', 'love'...

Q

Total questioning

—

"Can I ask a question?" said the man. "You just did!" said his companion, "but don't stop now - ask another..."

Questions, questions: the most valuable thing in business is a good question. The questions don't have to be 'big' to be important. Nor is it just about the number of questions, though that's nearer the mark. The Total Quality company simply maintains a climate, a culture, in which *everyone* asks questions *constantly*, at all levels, on all subjects, as a matter of course.

Q *Why aren't we doing it like that?*

Q *Why is 17 per cent of our raw material ending up as scrap?*

Q *What did we do that upset this customer so badly?*

Q *Do we really need a new machine for this, or can we adapt the one we've got?*

Q *Who would be the best people to make up a team to deal with this problem?*

   And so on...

And when the chips are down, the pressure is on, and the stakes are as high as they can be, what is the most natural, the most compelling, the most *human* response we can muster?

It's this:

> *"Everyone had this immense thirst for knowledge. Even the most junior people on the Squadron would question something, refusing to be fobbed off unless they were entirely happy: 'I don't agree. Why do it that way? Why not do it this way?' This attitude extended right down to even the smallest details of operational practice. With the prospect of death in front of them, people became much readier to question the wisdom of their superiors; and their superiors, on the whole, accepted this questioning as a healthy sign."*

Short quotation from *Tornado Down* by JOHN PETERS and JOHN NICHOL with WILLIAM PEARSON (Michael Joseph 1992) Copyright © John Peters and John Nichol, 1992. Reproduced by permission of Michael Joseph Ltd.

Answers are very important. Second in importance only to an inexhaustible flow of questions.

Q

Even when you have nine lives, there's no point in wasting one

"Jack Shewmaker, the former president of Wal-Mart, tells of going with Sam Walton, founder of the company and one of the richest men in America, into a competitor's store. The place was a total disaster, but instead of sneering and gloating his way through the aisles before stalking out, Walton noticed the one thing in the midst of all the chaos that was working for his rival and said, 'Jack, how come we're not doing that?'"

HENRY MACKAY, *Beware The Naked Man Who Offers You His Shirt* (1990) Piatkus Books

You can learn a lot from a cat.

Watch one sitting in its own garden. It's on familiar territory. It's at ease. But never is it entirely at rest. Watch the ears: constantly twitching, in search of a more effective position. A car door slamming in the distance; a gust of wind in the trees; the faraway bark of a dog: each sound brings an instant realignment of the ears, to get the best possible information.

The cat doesn't do this because it's been taught to. It isn't even conscious that it's doing it. It does it by instinct, unbeknown to itself.

What it's doing is maximising its chances of survival. Be alert; stay alive. Any noise may mean danger. Check it out, as best you possibly can.

That is what TQ demands of people: not clone-like obedience, as is so often imagined, but *aliveness*. Constant adaptation to the environment. Maximum use of the senses. Continuous, efficient and effective awareness of what's going on, leading to an appropriate response.

When your ears stop twitching, you're in mortal danger.

It's a matter of survival.

Total leadership

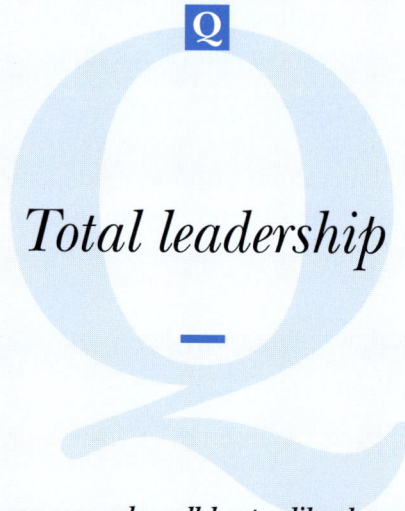

"...When the sea was calm, all boats alike showed mastership in floating."

WILLIAM SHAKESPEARE, *Coriolanus*

There's an old adage in the Royal Navy which says there are two kinds of ships: good ships, and bad ships. The difference between them is that good ships have good captains, and bad ships have bad captains.

Good captains lead. Their subordinates work hard and well and with dedication, not in the hope of reward or promotion, but simply to earn the respect of someone *they* respect. This sets the tone for the entire chain of command. Relations between the most junior officers and the hands tend to be good, positive, cheerful; everyone mucks in to get things done.

Bad captains give orders. Their subordinates do what they're told, because that's what you do if you receive an order. This sets the tone for the entire chain of command. It works, after a fashion. The ship still goes where the admiral orders it to go; it will still engage the enemy. But everyone on board is relieved when the ship docks and they can get the hell away from it all for a while.

In the SAS, the men elect their own officers. They don't elect the soft person, or the nice person, but the best person, the natural officer. People don't as a rule want a boss who makes their life easier. They want a leader.

Someone, crucially, who practises what they preach, because a leader who applauds initiative, drive and vision in his people while promoting time-servers will inevitably sow seeds of confusion, at best. Clarity, consistency and single mindedness are vital.

Perhaps the best single definition of leadership comes from one of the twentieth century's great leaders: Field Marshall Montgomery:

> *"The leader must have infectious optimism, and the determination to persevere in the face of difficulties. He must also radiate confidence, even when he himself is not too certain of the outcome. The final test of a leader is the feeling you have when you leave his presence after a conference. Have you a feeling of uplift and confidence?"*

Leadership. Hard to define; easy to recognise. And absolutely vital to the achievement of Total Quality.

"Welcome to 'You're Fired.' My first guest is an employee whose brand of fun-loving incompetence has been a delight to everyone in the company but me."

Q

It all begins with I contact

The potential is limitless. Liberating that potential is the essence of leadership. It all begins with what you might call 'I contact': basic, fundamental human contact between you and your people.

In his book, *Making it Happen,* John Harvey-Jones bemoans the stunted expectations companies tend to have of their people. They demand far too little of them. Without a challenge, people stop caring and it's when people stop caring that mistakes happen and accidents occur. Most people are capable of far more than they're ever asked for.

This is nowhere better illustrated than in companies' 'ageism'. The young are, all too often, ignored or patronised, despite all the evidence of their enormous capabilities, given the opportunity. As Harvey-Jones points out, in the 1939-45 war, he was second-in-command on a submarine at 19. His captain was 24.

In 1902, a 22-year-old was appointed 'technical expert third class' at the Swiss patent office. Three years later, working after office hours, he completed a paper on photoelectric effects (which would later bring him the Nobel prize), a doctoral thesis, a paper on Brownian motion and the Special Theory of Relativity. The following year, Albert Einstein was promoted to 'technical expert second class'.

The old tend to be treated even more shoddily: tacitly ignored until they have the good grace to shuffle off and retire. This despite the massive experience they possess and the degree of commitment they are willing to display.

According to Peters and Waterman, the single most important question facing organisations in the West is, 'What do you and your managers see – really *see* – when you look in the eye of a front-line employee?'

> **"Do you see a ne'er do well... who'd rip you off if you turned your back... who requires a 500-page rule book that tells you when to go to the bathroom? Or do you see a person who could literally fly to the moon without a face mask if only you would train the hell out of them, get the hell out of their way, and give them something worth doing"**
>
> Excerpt taken from *In Search of Excellence* by THOMAS J. PETERS and ROBERT H. WATERMAN JNR. Copyright © 1982 Thomas J. Peters and Robert H. Waterman Jnr. Reprinted by permission of HarperCollins Publishers Inc.

Once upon a time, being the boss meant having a big desk and a big office and big in-tray groaning with paperwork. Not in today's commercial climate. In the Total Quality company, being the boss means having a big dream, a big vision, and the ability to make sure that that vision is bought into, and supported, and pursued, at every level of the organisation.

It's a big challenge. But who ever said that being the boss was easy?

Q

'You're getting sleepy…sleepy…sleepy'

—

Ever seen a stage hypnotist?

A 21-year-old woman is put in a trance, and taken back to her sixth birthday party. She picks her nose. She sucks her hair. She talks and acts exactly the way a six-year-old would. 'What did you get for your birthday?' she's asked. 'I got a new bicycle with little wheels on the back and I got some chocolates and I got a colouring book and I got a doll's house and two new dolls.' Brought round from the trance, she's asked what she got for her sixth birthday. 'I don't know,' she says. 'We do,' replies the hypnotist…

A man is told to imagine that he is a solid steel bar. He goes totally rigid. He's then picked up, and laid like a bridge between two chairs: the back of his head on one, heels on another five feet away. A member of the audience is invited to come and sit on his stomach. He bears the weight effortlessly…

Moral: *we have capacities and capabilities we never dream of. We can do things we would never even think to attempt.*

Companies are much the same. The average organisation just isn't firing on all cylinders. Its people are bored, listless, demotivated; its managers too busy with internal power politics to talk to their colleagues or listen to their customers; its executives groaning with ulcers, or telling themselves they don't have a drink problem. But it doesn't have to be like this.

For personal fulfillment, people need a goal: challenging but achievable. For global best performance, companies need a goal: challenging but achievable.

The organisations which manage to offer their people challenging but achievable goals, whose attainment will also further the achievement of challenging but achievable corporate goals, will leave competitors gasping in their wake.

'What a piece of work is man,' said the bard. What a piece of work the turned-on organisation can be. It doesn't take hypnotism, but it's something of the same order. It's not by chance that great leaders are called 'spellbinding'.

The only limits are those we create for ourselves. Take off the shackles, release the energy, and watch your organisation fly! At last, you'll be *Jumping the Q!*

Q

"The significant problems we face cannot be solved at the same level of thinking we were at when we created them."

ALBERT EINSTEIN

Q

Bibliography

BROWN, M. (1989) *Richard Branson: The Inside Story Headline*

CARLZON, J. (1989) *Moments of Truth* HarperCollins Publishers Inc.

FORD, H. *My Life and Work* Doubleday, Page

HARVEY-JONES, J. (1988) *Making it Happen* Fontana

HEIDER, J. (1993) *The Tao of Leadership* Gower Publishing Group

IACOCCA, L. *Iacocca – An Autobiography* Sedgewick and Jackson

KAGAMI, H. (1993) in *International Management* Reed Business Publishing

KEEGAN, J. (1976) *The Face of Battle: Study of Agincourt, Waterloo and the Somme* Hutchinson

LOVE, J.F. (1986) *McDonald's: Behind the Arches* Bantam Books

MACKAY, H. (1990) *Beware the Naked Man Who Offers You His Shirt* Piatkus Books

MALCOLM, N. (1958) *Ludwig Wittgenstein: a Memoir* Oxford University Press

PETERS, J. AND J. NICHOL (1992) *Tornado Down* Michael Joseph

Peters, T. and R.H. Waterman Jnr (1982) *In Search of Excellence* HarperCollins Publishers Inc.

PIRSIG, R.M. (1991) *Zen and the Art of Motorcycle Maintenance* Bodley Head

RODDICK, A. (1992) *Body and Soul: How to Succeed in Business and Change the World* Vermilion

SIEFF, M. (1990) *On Management: Marks and Spencer Way* Weidenfeld and Nicholson

TERKEL, S. (1974) *Working* Pantheon Books

Q

KPMG

KPMG Peat Marwick is the UK practice of the world's largest accountancy and management consultancy firm KPMG. The origins of the UK firm date back to the 1860s and today its clients span the spectrum from multinational corporations, nationalised industries and government, to public and private businesses and individuals. The firm's professional services cover Audit and Accounting, Tax, Corporate Finance and Corporate Recovery and Management Consultancy.

KPMG's approach to Total Quality involves introducing our Quality Cycle into organisations in a way which is uniquely tailored to the culture and circumstances of each of our clients.

The KPMG Quality Cycle

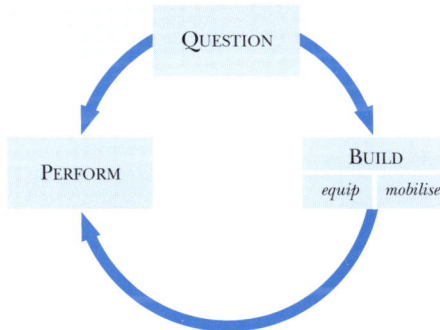

QUESTION

PERFORM

BUILD

equip *mobilise*

Copyright © 1992
KPMG Peat Marwick

The Cycle is linked to each organisation's annual business planning process. It ensures that strategic as well as operational aspects of Total Quality are addressed, and that people are not only able but also ready and willing to make the changes necessary for their organisation to succeed.

93

Q

Owen Bull is Head of Total Quality Consulting within KPMG Peat Marwick. He has 15 years' experience in international commerce, including time spent with Shell, Wellman Mechanical Engineering Ltd and Cincinnati Milacron.

In 1985 he joined a large consulting firm's strategic practice and was involved in strategic planning engagements with organisations such as British Aerospace, Unipart and Gulf Oil. He then became involved with change management and this culminated in his appointment in 1991 as European Sales Director for Total Quality consulting coupled with worldwide responsibility for the professional development of all the group's Total Quality consultants.

He joined KPMG Management Consulting in 1992, as Head of Total Quality Consulting and has since 1992 been building the firm's Quality practice. He is a regular speaker at international Quality conferences and writes for many of the leading magazines on Total Quality.

During this part of his consultancy career he has worked with many organisations, introducing the principles and practices of Total Quality. Clients have included British Telecom, Land Rover, Van den Burghs and Jurgens, PTT-Telecom Nederlands, British Aerospace, Midlands Electricity, Weston Park Hospital, The Insolvency Service and several Central Government Departments.

Q